"AND IT SHALL COME TO PASS IN THE LAST DAYS, SAITH GOD, I WILL POUR OUT MY SPIRIT UPON ALL FLESH...." ACTS 2:17

TO:

_____

FROM:

_____

DATE:

_____

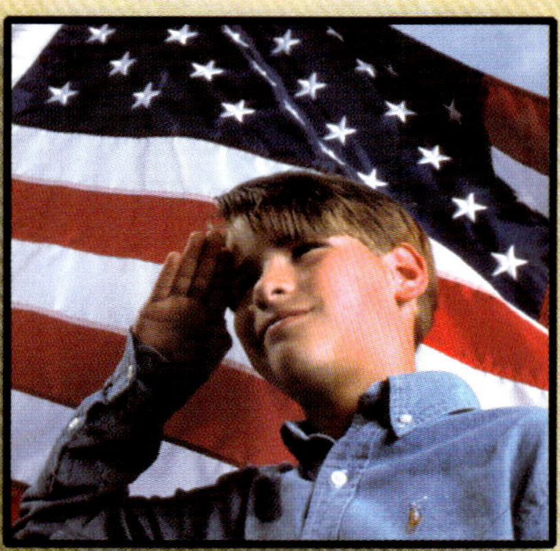

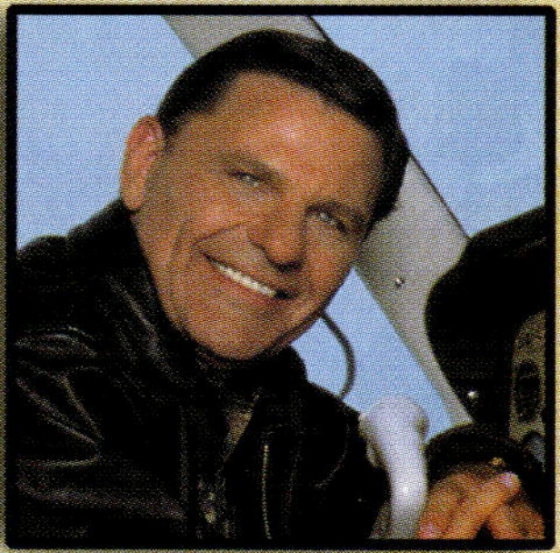

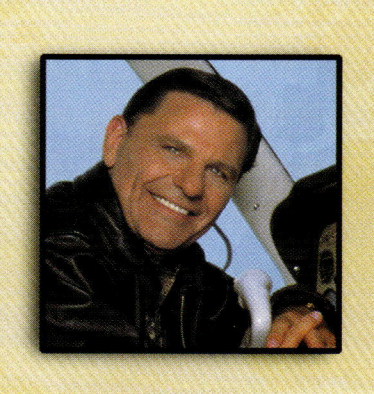

ONE NATION UNDER GOD

KENNETH COPELAND

Unless otherwise noted, all scripture is from the *King James Version* of the Bible.

Scripture quotations marked *New King James Version* are from the *New King James Version* © 1982 by Thomas Nelson, Inc.

One Nation Under God

ISBN 1-57562-676-4   30-0602

10 09 08 07 06 05 04 03 02   10 9 8 7 6 5 4 3 2 1

© 2002 Eagle Mountain International Church, Incorporated aka Kenneth Copeland Publications

Kenneth Copeland Publications

Fort Worth, Texas 76192-0001

For more information about Kenneth Copeland Ministries, call 1-800-600-7395 or visit www.kcm.org

Printed in the United States of America. All rights reserved under International Copyright Law. No part of this book may be reproduced or transmitted in any form or by any means, electronic or mechanical, including photocopying, recording, or by any information storage and retrieval system, without the written permission of the publisher.

KCP Records
The Music of Ministry

Produced by: Win Kutz

Executive Producers: Kenneth & Gloria Copeland

Live recording by: Ralph Robb

Engineered by: Win Kutz

Mixed by: Win Kutz

Assisted by: Robert Wirtz

Edited by: Robert Wirtz & Michael Howell

Piano: David Ellis

Organ: Wayne Stevens

Bass: Win Kutz

Guitar: Scott Allen

Drums: Jack Kelly

Percussion: Jim DeLong

Synth: Joe Ninowski

Background vocalists: Kathryn Glenn, Leah Luzecky, Wayne Stevens, Michael Howell, Robert Wirtz and Michael Phelps

Recorded Live at: The 2001 West Coast Believers' Convention in Anaheim, CA

Mastered by: Robert Wirtz at Eagle Mountain Recording Studio, Newark, Texas

Special Thanks To: Kenneth and Gloria Copeland

GOD BLESS AMERICA (INTRO)
Irving Berlin
(c) 1938 Irving Berlin Music Company. Williamson Music Company. Administered by The Harry Fox Agency.

AMERICA THE BEAUTIFUL
Catherine Lee Bates & Samuel A. Ward
Public Domain

GOD BLESS AMERICA
Irving Berlin
(c) 1938 Irving Berlin Music Company. Williamson Music Company. Administered by The Harry Fox Agency.

THE STAR SPANGLED BANNER
Francis Scott Key & John Stafford Smith
Public Domain

BATTLE HYMN OF THE REPUBLIC
Julia Ward Howe & William Steffe
Public Domain

THE STAR SPANGLED BANNER (REPRISE)
Francis Scott Key & John Stafford Smith
Public Domain

THE ARMY GOES ROLLING ALONG
Edmond L. Gruber, John Phillip Sousa
Public Domain

THE U.S. AIR FORCE
Robert Crawford
Publisher Unknown

ANCHORS AWEIGH
Domenico Savino & Charles A. Zimmerman
Public Domain

MARINES' HYMN
Author Unknown
Public Domain

GOD S DREAM OF A NATION

You've seen the pictures—boats filled with immigrants coming into New York Harbor with teary eyes fixed on the Statue of Liberty. That famous statue has been a symbol of economic opportunity and freedom from oppression for more than 200 years.

People are still looking for freedom. They are still seeking economic and political liberty. But more and more, they are looking for a freedom that runs much deeper.

In these last days, men and women from everywhere are going to flock by the boatloads, trainloads and planeloads to where they hear the Holy Ghost is being poured out. New people will gaze at that famous statue. As they look at it, they are going to say more than, "I'm in the land of the free." They are going to shout, "Hallelujah! I'm going to get free of this sickness and disease. I'm going to get free of this devil in me for the first time in my life. I'm coming to Jesus!"

That's because the nation to which they are coming will not be defined by geographical and political boundaries. They'll be seeking a nation within the nations. They'll be headed for the anointing. They'll be running to those who have become vessels for the outpouring of God's glory.

The nation they seek is a nation that has been in the heart of God since He first made covenant with Abraham: "Shall I hide from Abraham that thing which I do; Seeing that Abraham shall surely become a great and mighty nation, and all the nations of the earth shall be blessed in him?" (Genesis 18:17-18).

This dream shared by His people of every tribe and tongue is God's dream. It's a dream He would not hide from His covenant man, a dream He gave the promises of His covenant to fulfill. God's dream is to build a nation through whom all the nations of the earth would be blessed. That's been His dream from the beginning.

Who are the people of this nation within the nations? Every Spirit-filled believer willing to believe and receive all that has been made available to him through the promises of God's Word.

Where is this nation within the nations? Everywhere believers are standing immovable, confessing the eternal promises of God's Word as real until the temporary situations before them change to line up with what God has said.

God's dream is being fulfilled everywhere born-again, Spirit-filled, faith-talking believers are releasing the promises of His covenant into the earth. His people are the nation that is blessing all the nations of the earth.

—*Kenneth Copeland*

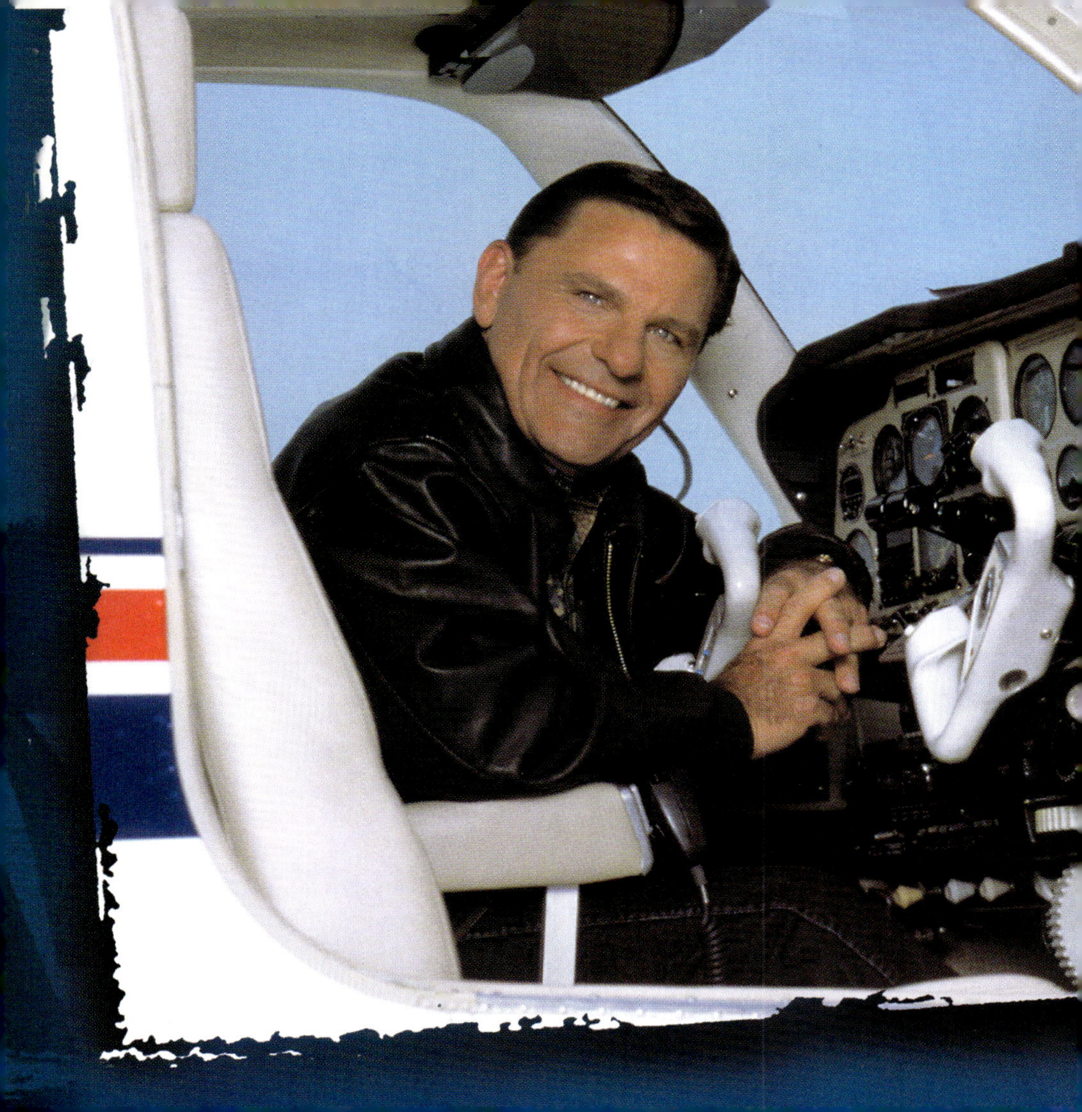

I PLEDGE ALLEGIANCE TO THE FLAG OF THE UNITED STATES OF AMERICA AND TO THE REPUBLIC FOR WHICH IT STANDS: ONE NATION UNDER GOD, INDIVISIBLE, WITH LIBERTY AND JUSTICE FOR ALL.

Pledge of allegiance

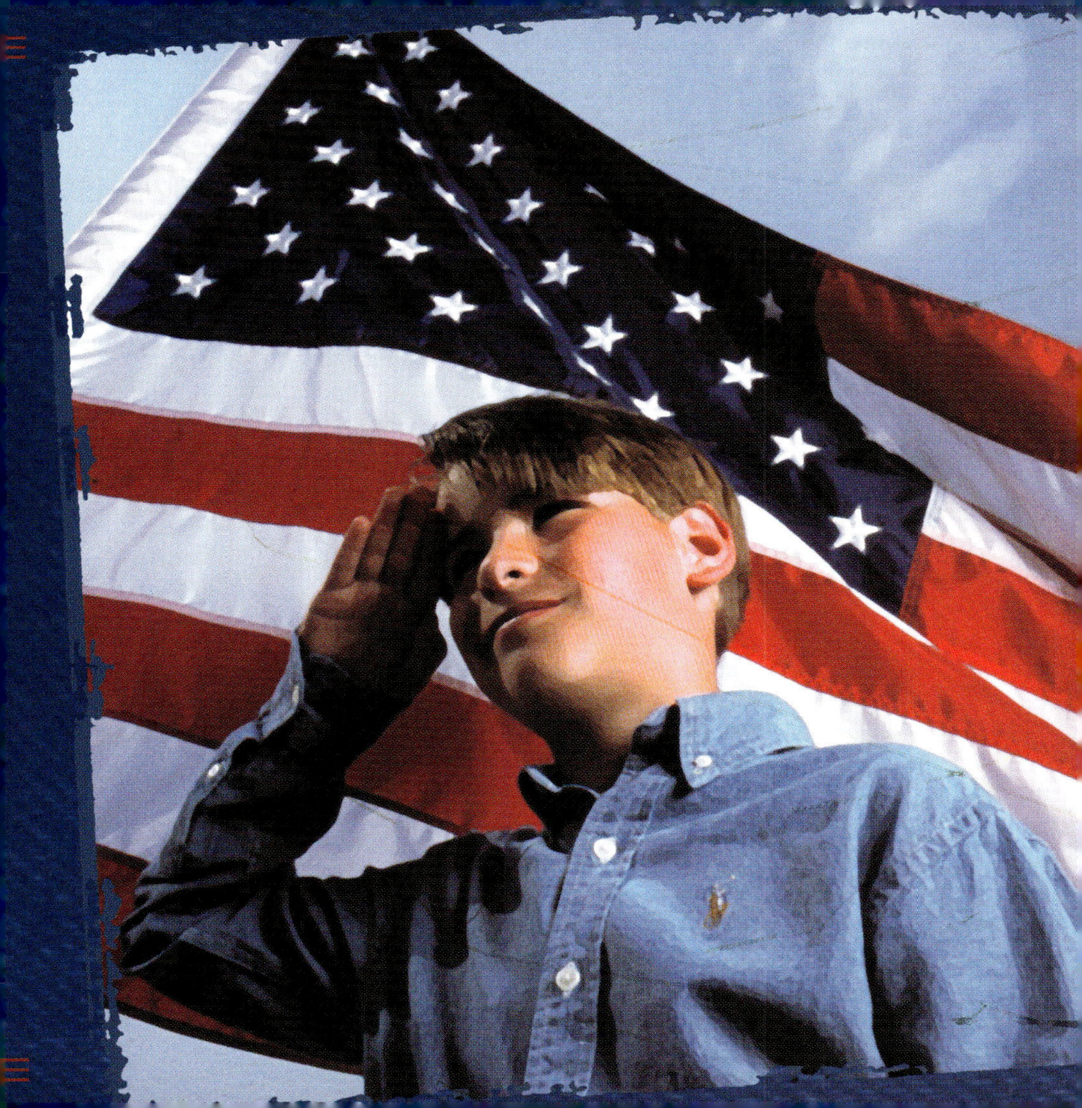

"If the Son therefore shall make you free, ye shall be free indeed."   John 8:36

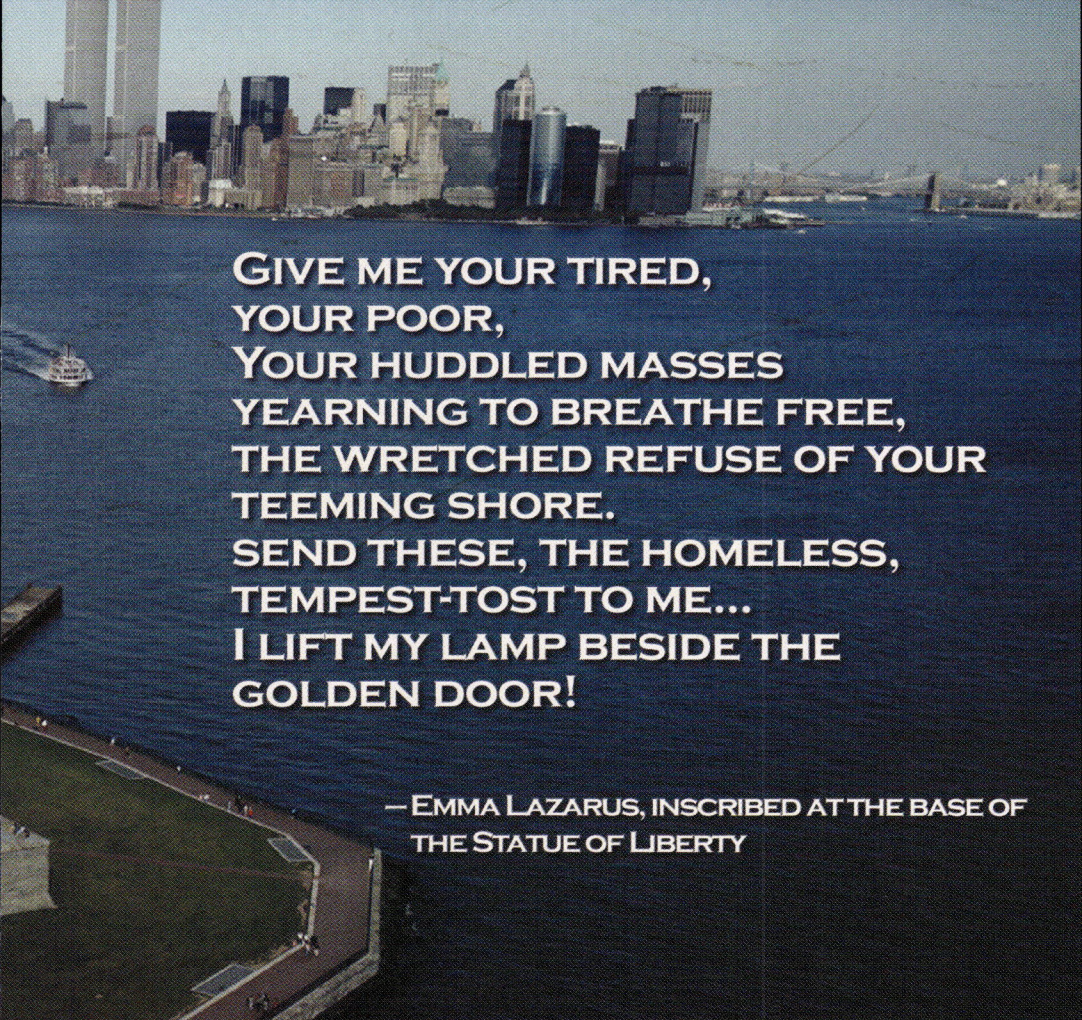

Give me your tired,
your poor,
Your huddled masses
yearning to breathe free,
the wretched refuse of your
teeming shore.
Send these, the homeless,
tempest-tost to me...
I lift my lamp beside the
golden door!

—Emma Lazarus, inscribed at the base of the Statue of Liberty

> WE HOLD THESE TRUTHS TO BE SELF EVIDENT THAT ALL MEN ARE CREATED EQUAL. THAT THEY ARE ENDOWED BY THEIR CREATOR WITH CERTAIN INALIENABLE RIGHTS THAT AMONG THESE ARE LIFE, LIBERTY AND THE PURSUIT OF HAPPINESS....
>
> THE DECLARATION OF INDEPENDENCE

Two hundred and twenty-five years ago, a document was written and signed, the likes of which did not exist in government before that time. It stated unashamedly that God had obviously given priceless worth to every person. Not just kings or nobles or people singled out for special treatment. No, everyone. Where did this world-shaking idea come from—the priceless importance of the human individual? It can be found only in the heart of Almighty God.

IS IT NOT THAT IN THE *chain of human events, the birthday of the nation is* **INDISSOLUBLY LINKED** *with the birthday of the Savior. That the* **DECLARATION OF INDEPENDENCE** *laid the cornerstone of human government upon the* **FIRST PRECEPTS OF CHRISTIANITY.**

—John Quincy Adams

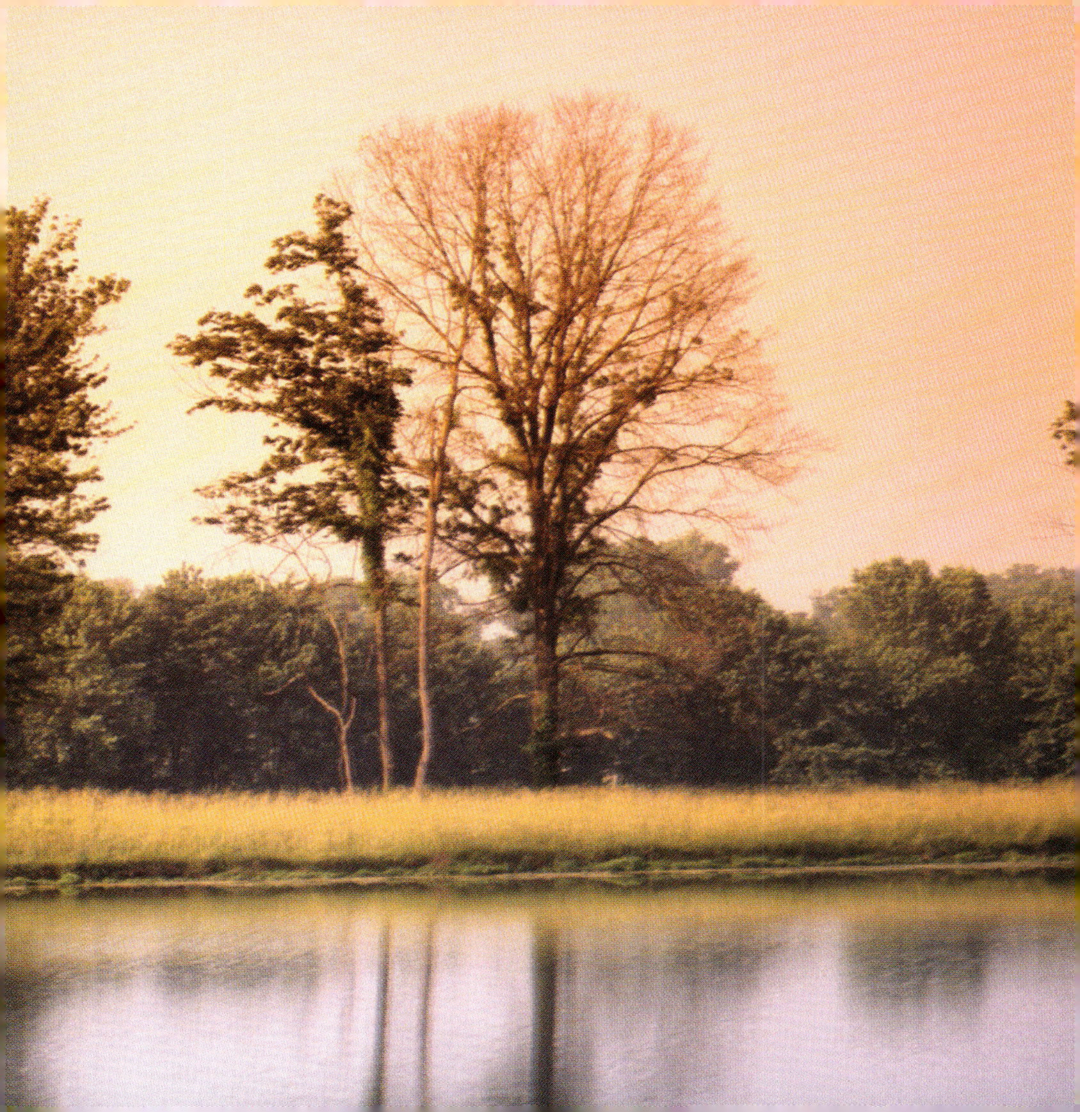

GOD'S PLAN AND GOD ARE NOT GOING TO BE DENIED.

We are going to fulfill our destiny. We are going to release the glory of God that has been incubated here, that has been growing here, that has been developing here for hundreds of years.

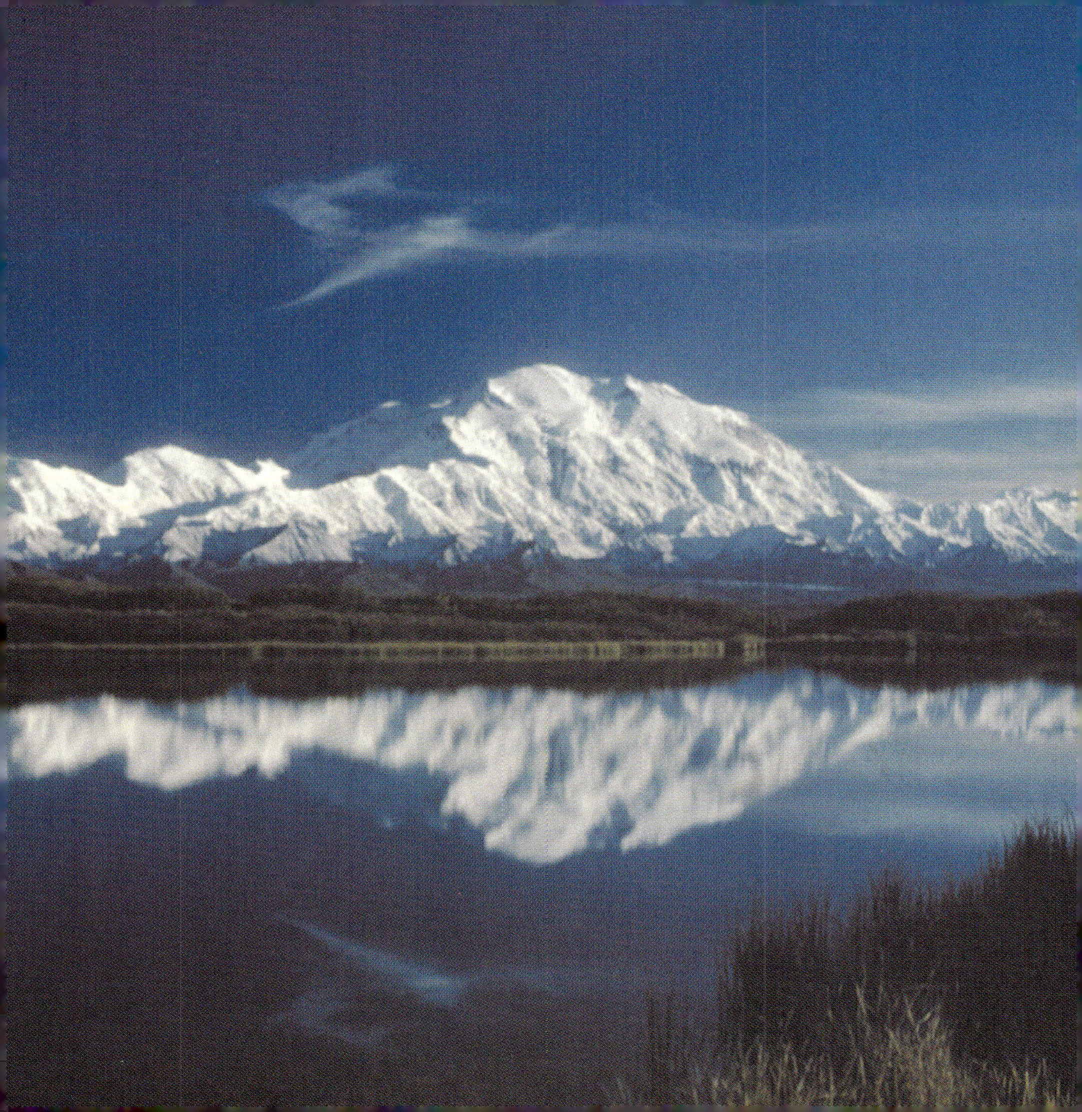

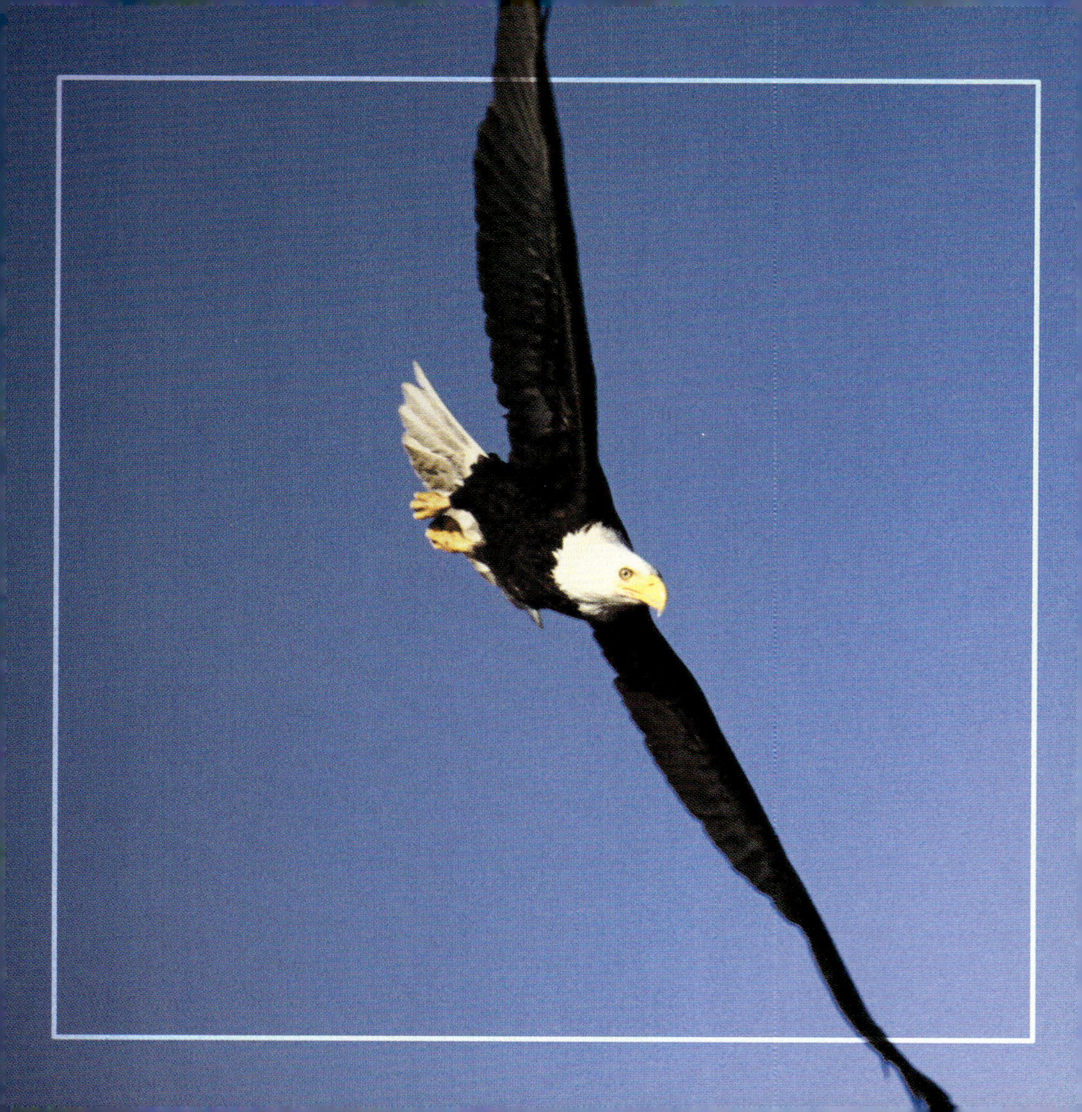

ONE NATION UNDER GOD

KENNETH COPELAND

KENNETH
COPELAND
PUBLICATIONS
FORT WORTH, TEXAS

Prayer For God's Dream To Be Fulfilled

Father, You said that in Your dream all nations would be blessed by Your nation. We give ourselves to You once again, and in the Name of Jesus, we're doing our best to turn from our wicked ways. You said if Your people called by Your Name would do that, then You would hear from heaven and heal our land. And we believe that the land is being healed.

I ask You, Father, to bring such an outpouring of Your glory that men and women will once again begin to see that this is Your dream that we're living in the midst of—that the milk and the honey that flows here—is to help build Your dream and to help meet the needs of the people.

Today, Father, we recommit ourselves to look unto You and unto heaven for that dream, in the Name of Jesus.

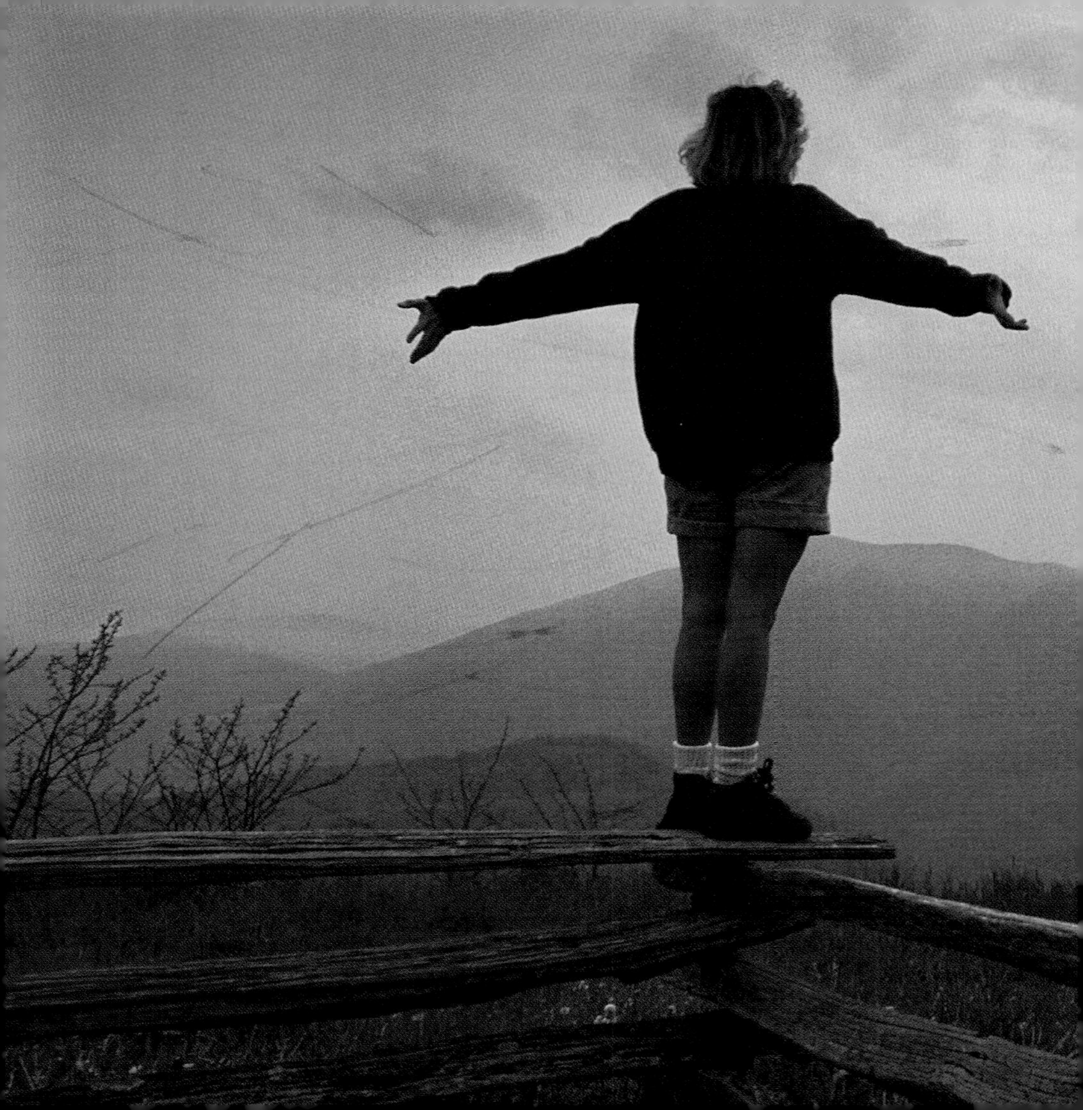

"BUT YE ARE A CHOSEN GENERATION, A ROYAL PRIESTHOOD, AN HOLY NATION, A PECULIAR PEOPLE; THAT YE SHOULD SHOW FORTH THE PRAISES OF HIM WHO HATH CALLED YOU OUT OF DARKNESS INTO HIS MARVELOUS LIGHT: WHICH IN TIME PAST WERE NOT A PEOPLE, BUT NOW ARE THE PEOPLE OF GOD...." 1 PETER 2:9-10

"Go therefore and make disciples of all the nations, baptizing them in the name of the Father and of the Son and of the Holy Spirit."

Matthew 28:19, *New King James Version*

It has *always* been God's plan to have a nation where the glory of God could be *sown and nurtured,* from which His glory could spread throughout the *whole earth*—where all people could praise the *God of heaven* and be protected from *sin, sickness, demons, fear and disease and all the curse* that had come on this earth.

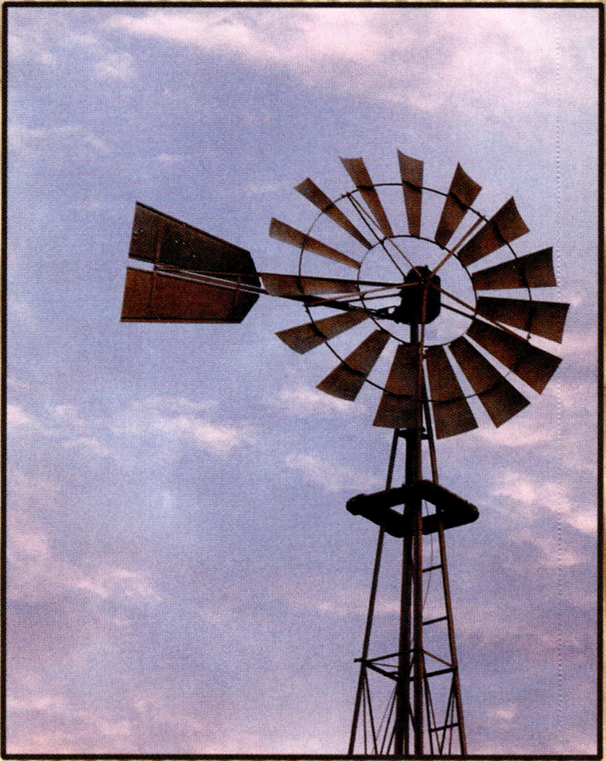

"If my people, which are called by my name, shall humble themselves, and pray, and seek my face, and turn from their wicked ways; then will I hear from heaven, and will forgive their sin, and will heal their land."

2 Chronicles 7:14

Think about it...

a nation filled with the fire of God, the power of God, the resurrection of His power and presence and the honor of the Most High God, and from that place there could come a presence of God and spill out all over this planet, all over this whole world. God set out to build a nation like that where the glory would reside. The Bible said that God inhabits the praises of His people and His glory is in His presence. So it would have to be a nation where *all people could freely praise and worship Him.*

"But as truly as I live, all the earth shall be filled with the glory of the Lord."

Numbers 14:21

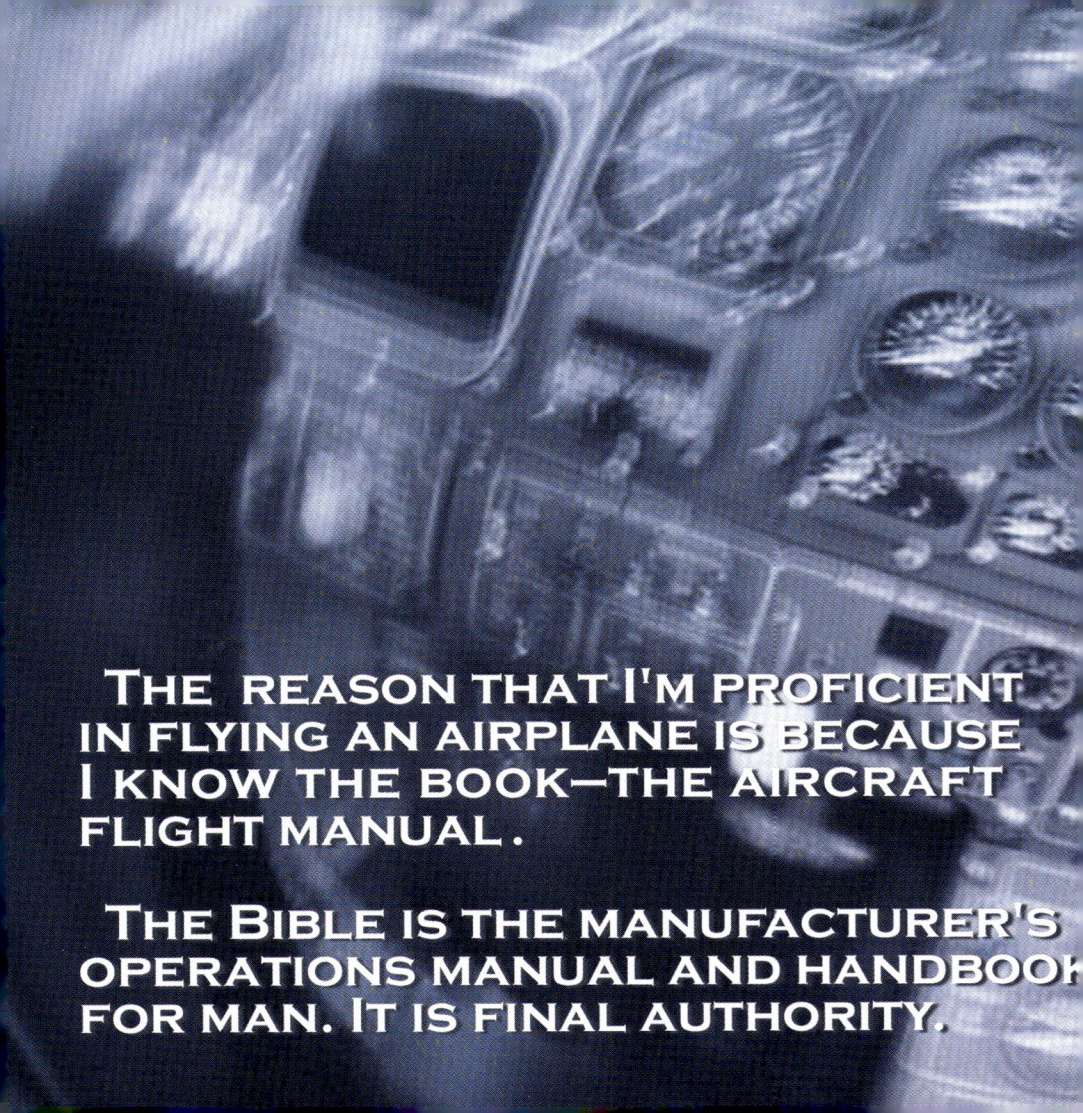

The reason that I'm proficient in flying an airplane is because I know the book—the aircraft flight manual.

The Bible is the manufacturer's operations manual and handbook for man. It is final authority.

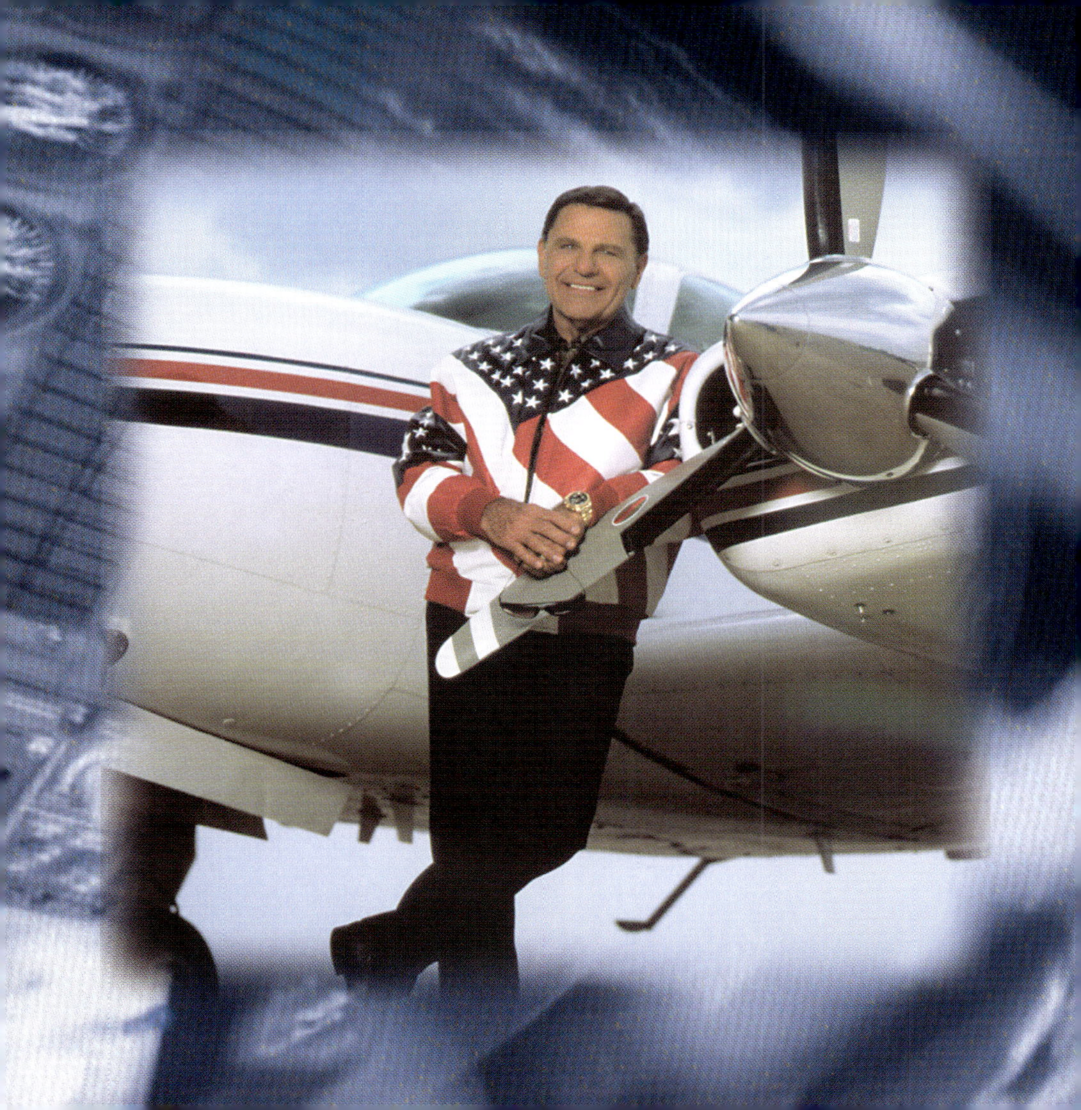

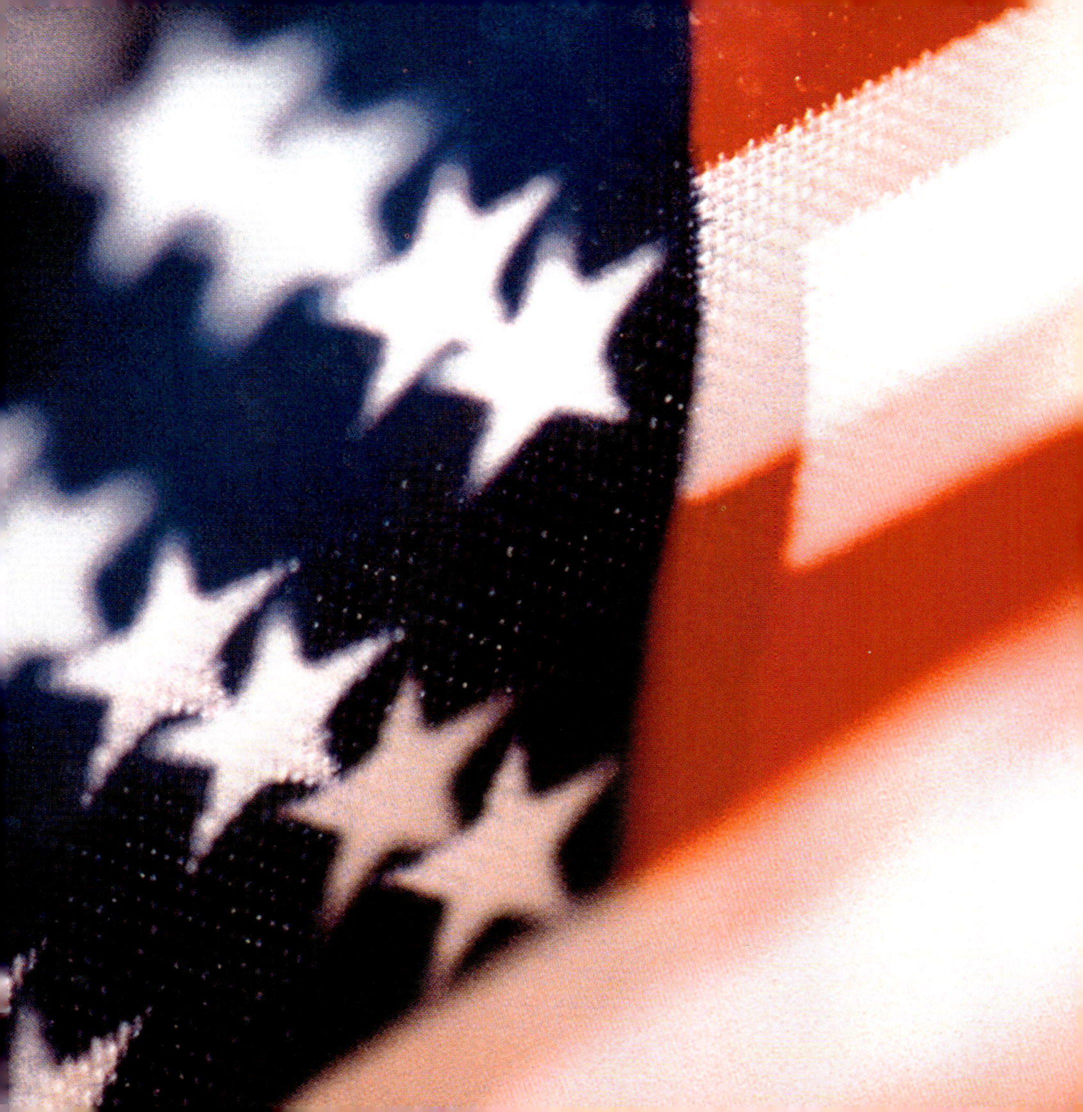

The American dream is God's Dream— one nation under God **filled with His glory.**

This is God's place—

the incubator of His Glory.

Even our flag is called Old Glory.

O, say does that star-spangled banner yet wave O'er the land of the free and the home of the brave?

From *The Star Spangled Banner* by Francis Scott Key

This flag is not a political symbol.

It doesn't represent a political party. It represents a mighty, free people, the freest people on the face of the earth. It represents all that is good and sacred and godly in this country. THIS FLAG represents the blood of Jesus and the purity of the new birth and the Word of God.

Holy Bible

GOD IS A COVENANT-MAKING GOD. GOD DOES NOT DO ANYTHING IN THIS EARTH ANYWHERE, ANY TIME WITHOUT A COVENANT.

"IN THE NAME OF GOD, AMEN.
WE, WHOSE NAMES ARE UNDERWRITTEN...
HAVING UNDERTAKEN FOR THE GLORY OF GOD,
AND ADVANCEMENT OF THE CHRISTIAN FAITH...
A VOYAGE TO PLANT THE FIRST COLONY IN THE
NORTHERN PARTS OF VIRGINIA...."

THE MAYFLOWER COMPACT

A tiny little ship came to the shores of this continent. It was called the Mayflower. The people aboard had the glory of God in their bosom and a prayer of faith in their hearts for a place where they could worship God in freedom. On board that vessel these people entered into a covenant with God to establish the land of His dreams in the Name and in the blood of Jesus Christ of Nazareth.

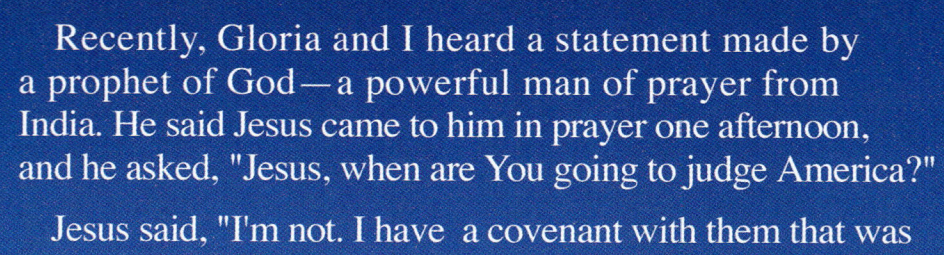

Recently, Gloria and I heard a statement made by a prophet of God—a powerful man of prayer from India. He said Jesus came to him in prayer one afternoon, and he asked, "Jesus, when are You going to judge America?"

Jesus said, "I'm not. I have a covenant with them that was made on the Mayflower, and I remember that covenant...."

God has a covenant that He made with 200 of His saints who came over here on the Mayflower. They established a covenant in the blood of Jesus that eventually gave birth to a nation. It has saved that nation over and over. God will not forget that covenant.

Gulf of Mexico
Atlanta
Jacksonville
Tampa
Orlando
Key West
Miami
Havana
THE BAHAMAS
CUBA
JAMAICA
BELIZE
Guatemala
GUATEMALA
EL SALVADOR
Tegucigalpa
HONDURAS
HAITI
NICARAGUA
Managua
San Jose
COSTA RICA
PANAMA
Caribbean
VENEZUELA
ECUADOR
Mexico City
Monterrey

IT CANNOT BE EMPHASIZED TOO STRONGLY OR TOO OFTEN THAT THIS GREAT NATION WAS FOUNDED NOT BY RELIGIONISTS, BUT BY CHRISTIANS, NOT ON RELIGIONS, BUT ON THE GOSPEL OF JESUS CHRIST.

—PATRICK HENRY

FREEDOM
TO WORSHIP AND PRAISE GOD HAS NEVER BEEN CHEAP. IT COST JESUS HIS LIFE. IT COST A LOT OF OTHER PEOPLE THEIR LIVES.

— Kenneth Copeland

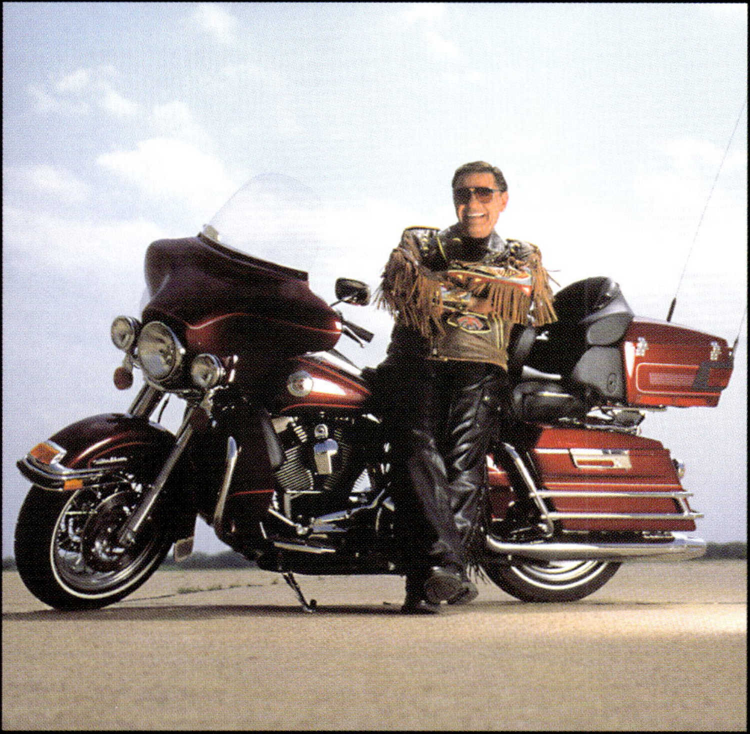

"The thief cometh not, but for to steal, and to kill, and to destroy: I am come that they might have life, and that they might have it more abundantly." John 10:10

These acts of mass murder were intended to frighten our nation into chaos and retreat. But they have failed. Our country is strong. A great people has been moved to defend a great nation.

Terrorist attacks can shake the foundations of our biggest buildings, but they cannot touch the foundation of America. These acts shatter steel, but they cannot dent the steel of American resolve.

America was targeted for attack because we're the brightest beacon for freedom and opportunity in the world. And no one will keep that light from shining.

— President George W. Bush
September 11, 2001

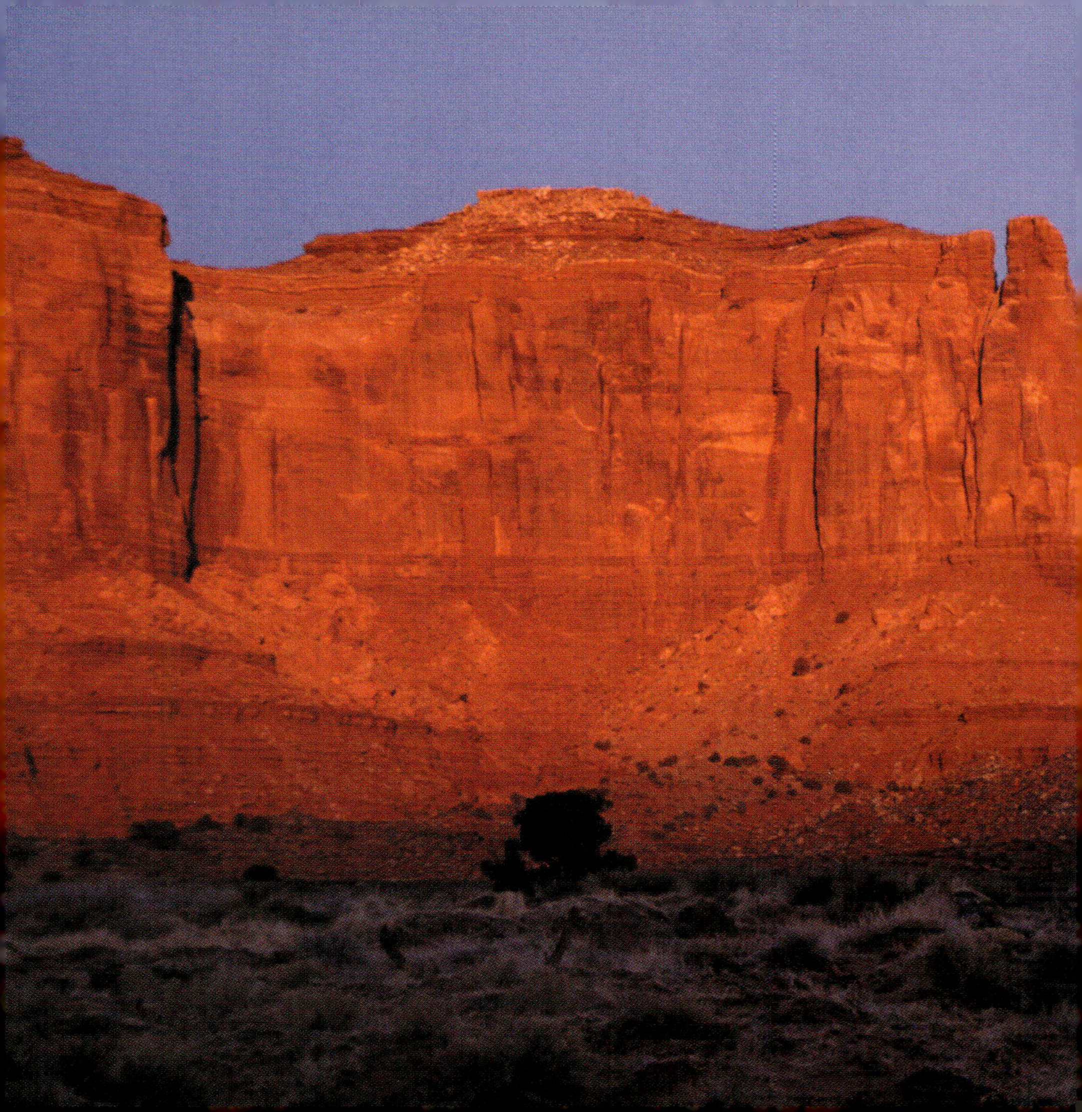

" *Thou art my Son; this day have I begotten thee. Ask of me, and I shall give thee the heathen for thine inheritance, and the uttermost parts of the earth for thy possession.*"   Psalm 2:7-8

"And as the Berlin Wall fell in one day, churches will be overflowed in one day. As all of Eastern Europe changed in one day, whole nations will come to Me in one day, saith the Lord. I am the God that created nations and I am the God that is their Savior."

Prophecy given through Kenneth Copeland
Fort Worth, Texas, January 19, 1994

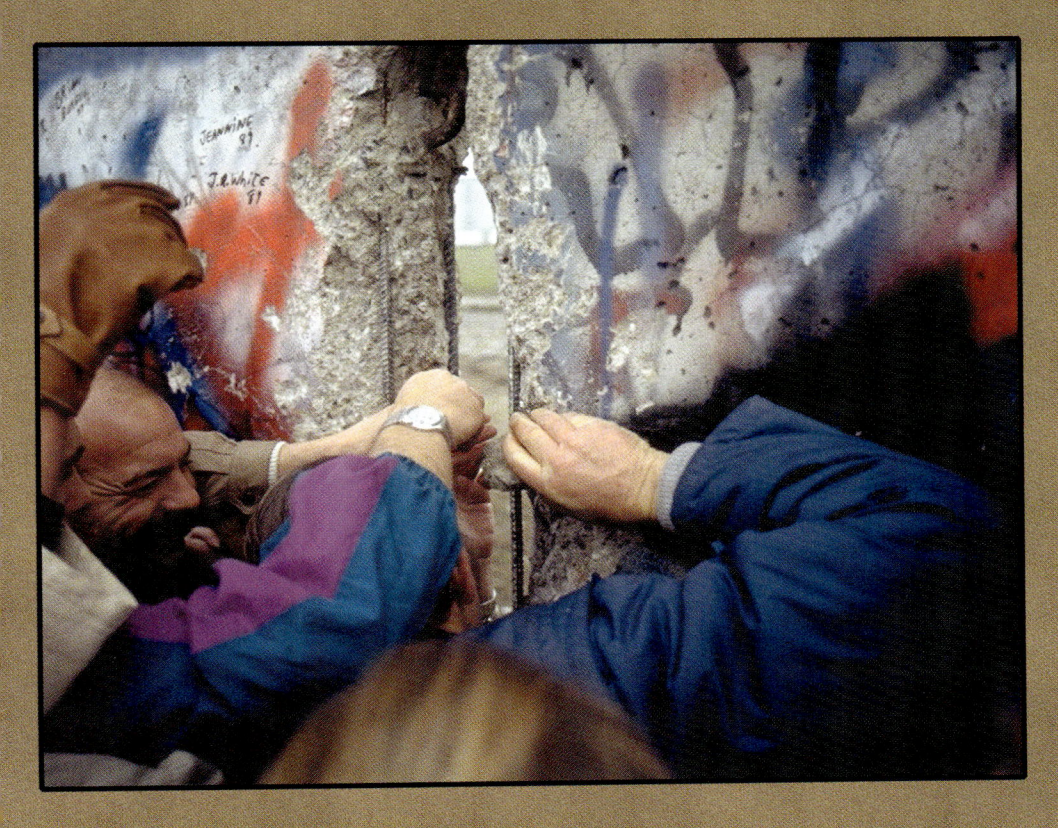

"Yea, all kings shall fall down before him: all nations shall serve him."
Psalm 72:11

"FOR GOD SO LOVED THE WORLD, THAT HE GAVE HIS ONLY BEGOTTEN SON, THAT WHOSOEVER BELIEVETH IN HIM SHOULD NOT PERISH, BUT HAVE EVERLASTING LIFE." JOHN 3:16

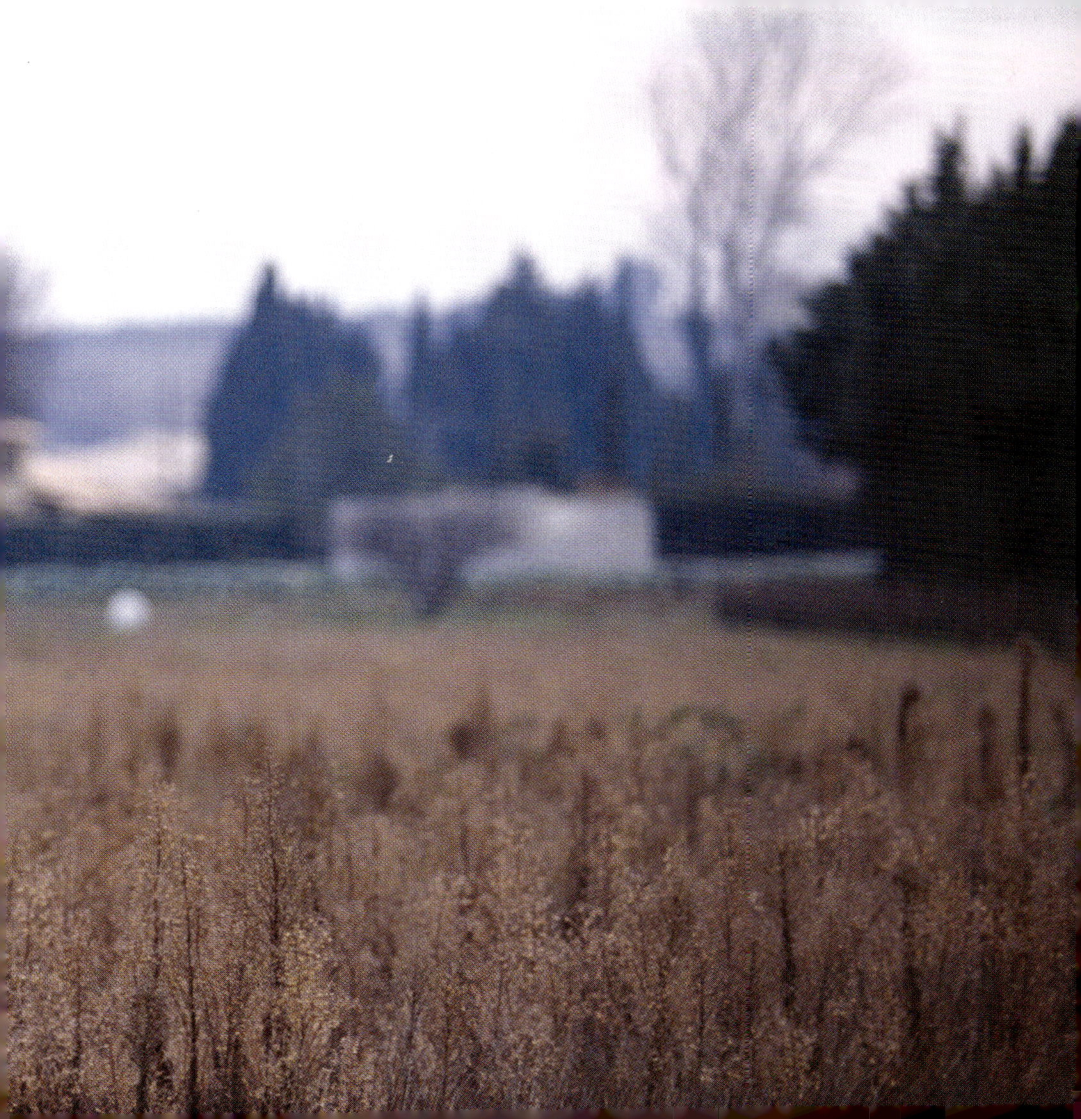

I don't care where you are in this world, the Holy Ghost is there. You can get born again anywhere on this planet standing in any spot, any hour of the day or night.

"Whosoever shall call on the name of the Lord shall be saved!" Acts 2:21

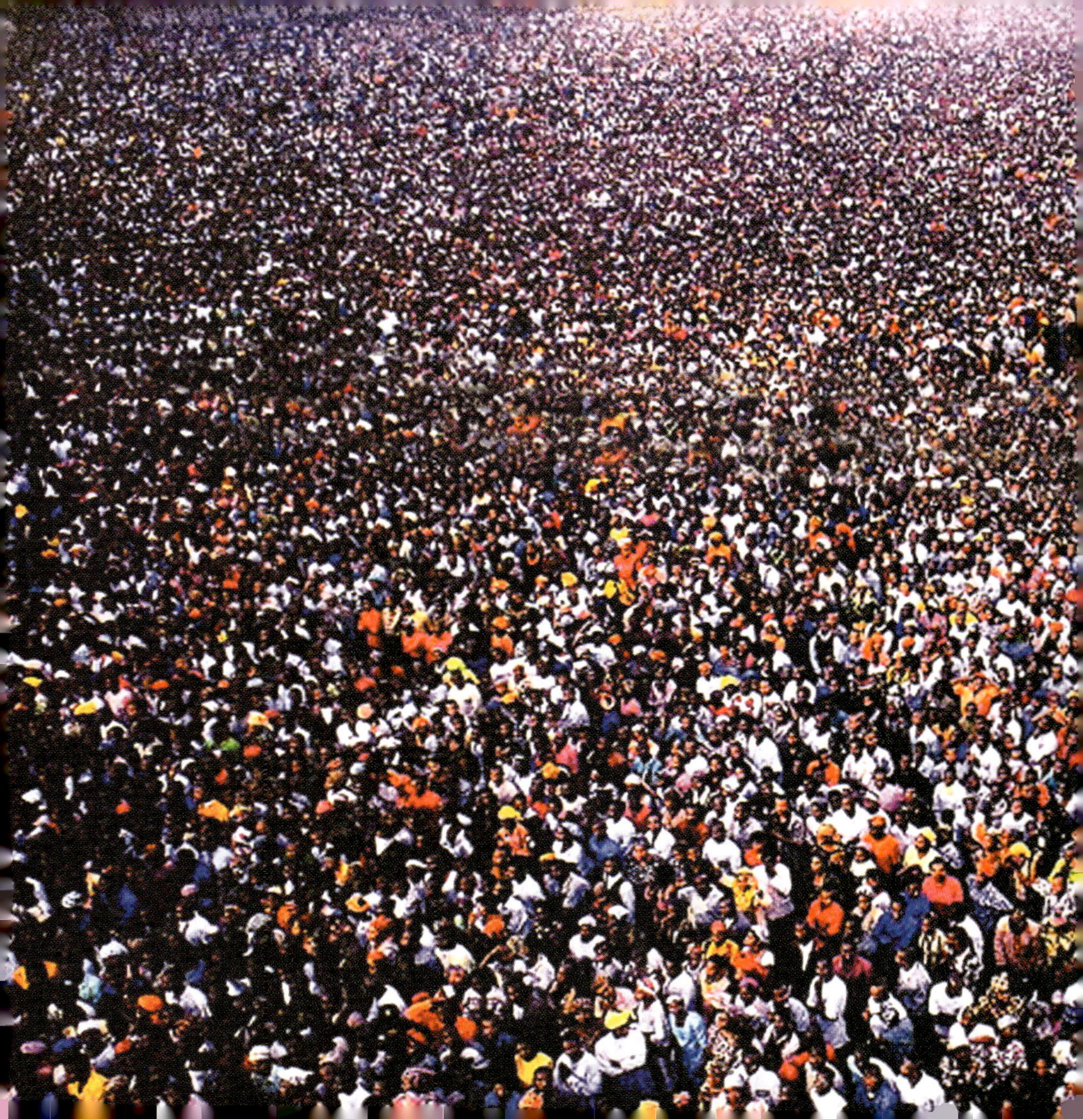

1,093,475
People Receive Salvation!

In 1984, just before we dedicated our first big gospel tent in South Africa, I was sitting in a trailer next to the tent when there was a knock on the door—it was Kenneth Copeland. After a wonderful time of fellowship, he began to prophesy. He said, *"The day will come when you'll see a million people saved in one service."*

On November 12, 2000, the final night of the Lagos, Nigeria, crusade, that prophecy was fulfilled—1,093,475 people received salvation! By the end of this six-day crusade in Lagos, *six million people registered to hear the gospel!*

When I read the crusade statistics, tears flowed from my eyes. It was prophecy fulfilled.

—Reinhard Bonnke
March 11, 2001

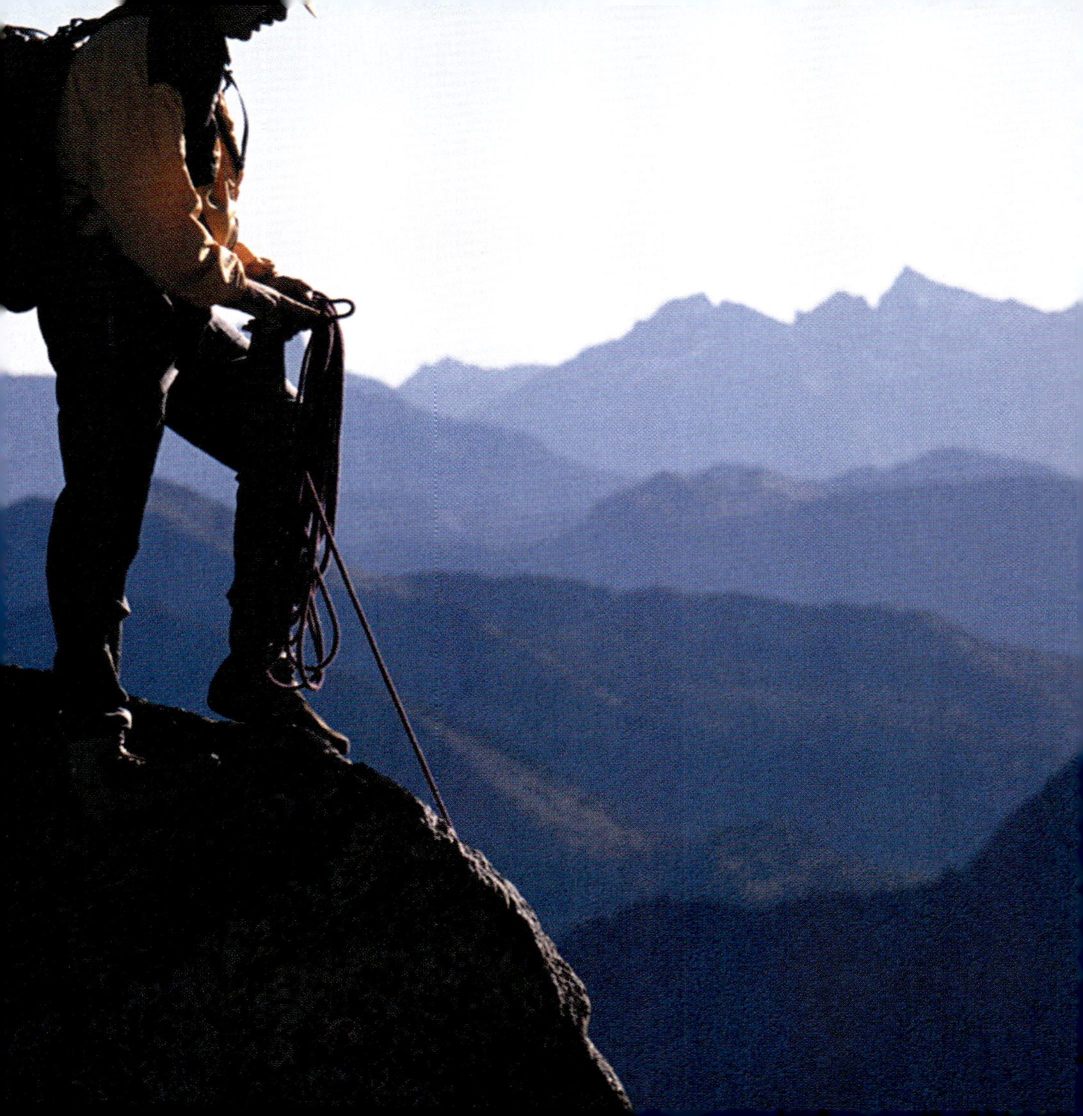

"AND YE SHALL KNOW THE TRUTH, AND THE TRUTH SHALL MAKE YOU FREE." JOHN 8:32

"Ye that go down to the sea, and all that is therein; the isles, and the inhabitants thereof. Let the wilderness and the cities thereof lift up their voice...let the inhabitants of the rock sing, let them shout from the top of the mountains. Let them give glory unto the Lord, and declare his praise in the islands."

— Isaiah 42:10-12

In 1995, Brother Copeland, Jerry Savelle and Jesse Duplantis were flying over the South Pacific when the Lord commissioned them to go to the islands of the world. The three men then remembered a prophecy spoken by Smith Wigglesworth that the islands of the world would be among the last places where a great outpouring of God's glory would manifest before Jesus' return.

Anybody anywhere can have hope if they KNOW JESUS and the covenant promises of **GOD.**

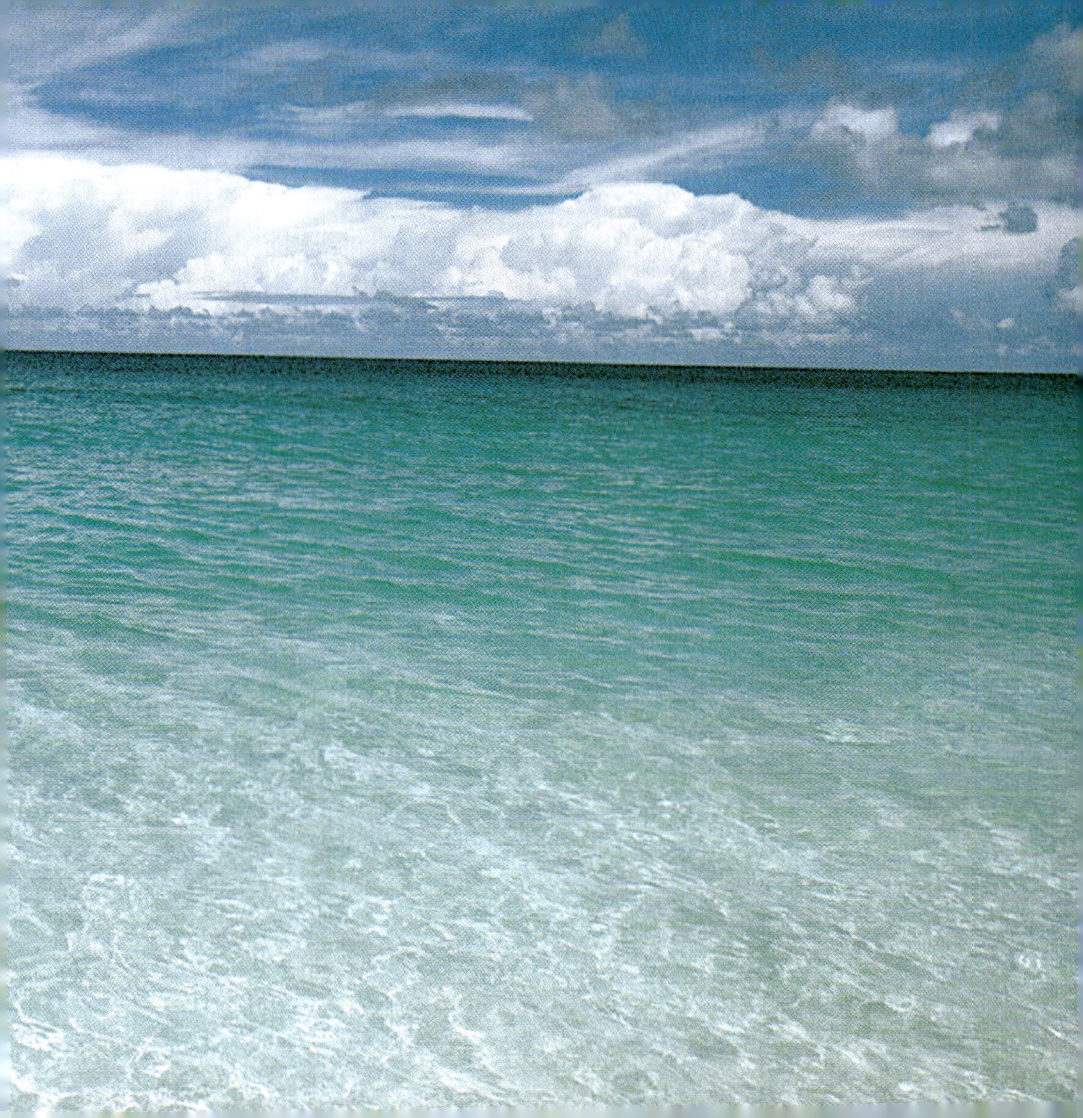

"...These are those days, saith the Lord. I am healing the wounds! On both sides. There will be forgiveness that will look and sound so strange, particularly to white men's ears....There are some yet in this government that had almost rather die than to apologize to the red man. But they'll do it anyway. And you're going to hear it. And you're going to see it. And you're going to say, "My, my, my, the Lord told us that was going to happen!" There are going to be public apologies, because it is My Spirit and I said they would...."

Prophecy given through Kenneth Copeland, September 20, 1995, Minneapolis Victory Campaign

Let us begin by expressing our profound sorrow for what this agency has done in the past. Just like you, when we think of these misdeeds and their tragic consequences, our hearts break and our grief is as pure and complete as yours. We desperately wish that we could change this history, but of course we cannot.

On behalf of the Bureau of Indian Affairs, I extend this formal apology to Indian people for the historical conduct of this agency.

—Kevin Gover, Assistant Secretary
Bureau of Indian Affairs
September 8, 2000

OUR GLORY...

Our glory has never been in our military might. Our glory has certainly never been in our brilliant politics. Our glory has been in our people who pray. Our glory has been in the Name of the Lord Jesus Christ of Nazareth and standing on His Word. We're still standing there and **He's still God, and He's still Lord of this nation.**

ONE PERSON WITH FAITH, COURAGE AND GOD MAKES A MAJORITY.

— KENNETH COPELAND

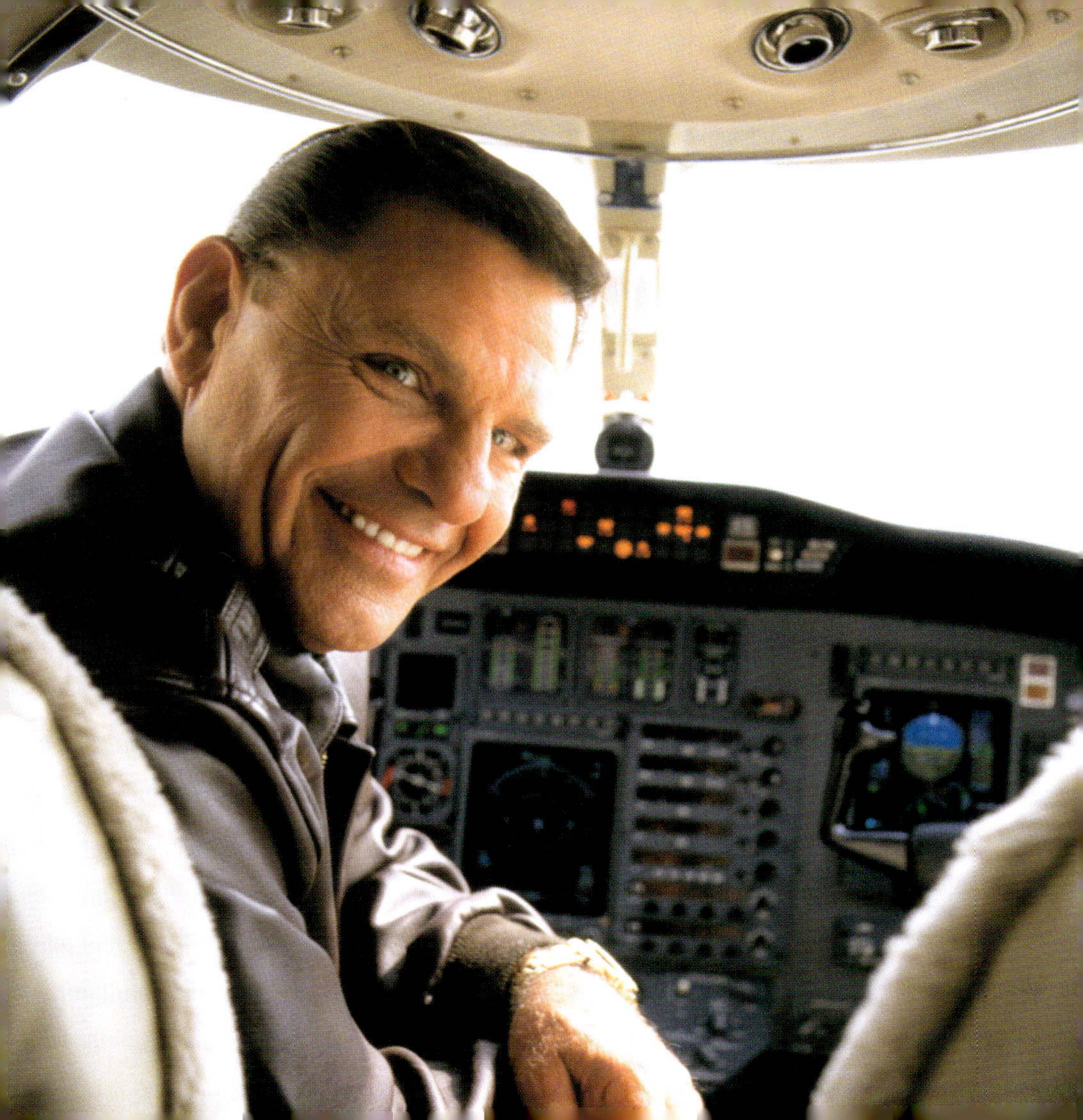

A PRAYER FOR THE NATIONS

Daily, international events are setting the stage for Jesus' return. As believers in every land continue to pray on behalf of their leaders, God is pouring out of His Spirit, making tremendous power available to guide the governments of every nation according to His divine will and plan. As you stand for your nation, you can pray the following:

Oh God in heaven, I come before You in the Name of Jesus on behalf of the leaders of this nation. You said the heart of the king is in Your hand and You will turn it whichever way You choose (Proverbs 21:1). I ask You to direct the heart and mind of (the name of your nation's leader) to make decisions that will lead our country in Your ways and according to Your Word.

I thank You, Lord, for bringing change to the politics of our nation. Thank You for changing the voices of influence to speak in agreement with Your Word. I ask You to send laborers filled with the spirit of wisdom and might, to surround our leaders with godly counsel and insight. I also ask You to remove from positions of authority those who stubbornly oppose righteousness, and replace them with men and women who will follow You and Your appointed course for (the name of your nation).

As we enter the final hours of the last days, I ask for the spirit of faith, the workings of miracles, for signs, wonders, gifts, and demonstrations of the Holy Spirit and power to be in strong operation. Let believers in (the name of your nation) and in every land be unified to stand strong by faith in Jesus, the Anointed One and His Anointing, that Your glory may be revealed in all the earth.

Thank You, Lord, that these requests come to pass. I believe I receive. Amen.

PRAYER FOR SALVATION AND BAPTISM IN THE HOLY SPIRIT

Heavenly Father, I come to You in the Name of Jesus. Your Word says, "Whosoever shall call on the name of the Lord shall be saved" (Acts 2:21). I am calling on You. I pray and ask Jesus to come into my heart and be Lord over my life according to Romans 10:9-10. "If thou shalt confess with thy mouth the Lord Jesus, and shalt believe in thine heart that God hath raised him from the dead, thou shalt be saved. For with the heart man believeth unto righteousness; and with the mouth confession is made unto salvation." I do that now. I confess that Jesus is Lord, and I believe in my heart that God raised Him from the dead.

I am now reborn! I am a Christian—a child of Almighty God! I am saved! You also said in Your Word, "If ye then, being evil, know how to give good gifts unto your children: HOW MUCH MORE shall your heavenly Father give the Holy Spirit to them that ask him?" (Luke 11:13). I'm also asking You to fill me with the Holy Spirit. Holy Spirit, rise up within me as I praise God. I fully expect to speak with other tongues as You give me the utterance (Acts 2:4). In Jesus Name. Amen!

Begin to praise God for filling you with the Holy Spirit. Speak those words and syllables you receive—not in your own language, but the language given to you by the Holy Spirit. You have to use your own voice. God will not force you to speak. Don't be concerned with how it sounds. It is a heavenly language!

Continue with the blessing God has given you and pray in the spirit every day.

You are a born-again, Spirit-filled believer. You'll never be the same!

Find a good Word of God preaching church, and become a part of a church family who will love and care for you as you love and care for them.

We need to be connected to each other. It increases our strength in God. It's God's plan for us.

At Pentecost, a new nation was born—a nation of reborn men and women, empowered by the Holy Spirit to believe and receive and minister the blessings of covenant with God, vessels through whom His glory would fill the earth.